A BOOK A

_____

Photo
3X5

PREPARED WITH LOVE BY

_____

"Love bears all things, believes
all things, hopes all things,
endures all things."

−1 Corinthians 13:7

Before you arrived

Due Date

"You formed my inmost being; you knit me in my mother's womb."

-Psalm 139:13

WE PRAY YOU...

LOVE _____

ALWAYS _____

NEVER _____

GROW TO BE _____

FIND JOY IN _____

Dear God,
    Wrap this dear child in your protection. Pour out your love, providing happiness, health and safety.

THE STORY BEHIND YOUR NAME

_____

_____

_____

_____

YOUR PATRON SAINT

_____

Pray for this child!

THE DAY YOU WERE BORN

DATE:

TIME:

DOCTOR:

HOSPITAL:

LENGTH:

WEIGHT:

HAIR COLOR:

EYE COLOR:

"I praise you, because I am wonderfully made."

–Psalm 139:14

Your Footprints

"Your word is a lamp for my feet, a light for my path."

-Psalm 119:105

BAPTISM

"Go, therefore, and make disciples
of all nations, baptizing them
in the name of the Father, and of
the Son, and of the Holy Spirit."

-Matthew 28:19

BAPTIZED BY	DATE	CHURCH	GODPARENT(S)

"Let the children come to me."

–Mark 10:14

YOUR FIRST

 MASS

 PILGRIMAGE

Photo
2X3

Photo
2X3

 CHRISTMAS

 EASTER

Photo
2X3

Photo
2X3

_____

Laugh

_____

Tooth

_____

Solid Food

Smile

_____

"When I smiled on them
they could not believe it."
-Job 29:24

_____

Word

_____

Haircut

_____

Time Sleeping through the Night

Step

_____

"Nothing gives me greater joy
than to hear that my children
are walking in the truth."
-3 John 1:4

YOU GREW & GREW...

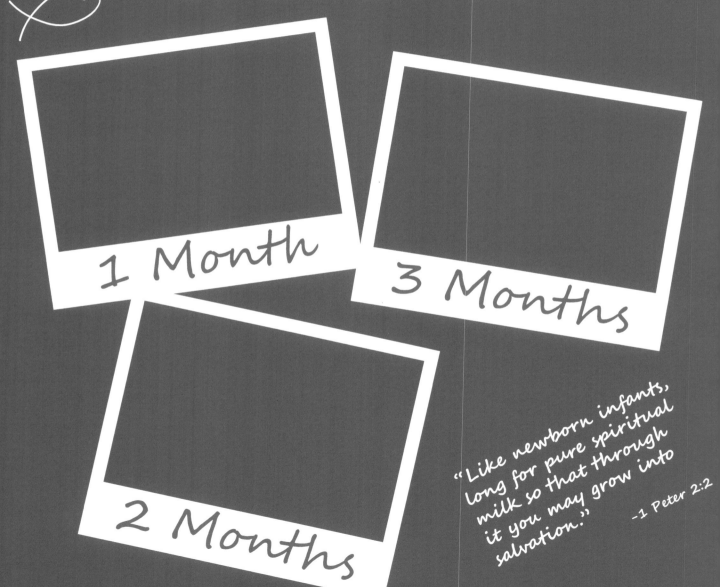

1 Month

3 Months

2 Months

"Like newborn infants, long for pure spiritual milk so that through it you may grow into salvation." —1 Peter 2:2

4 Months

5 Months

6 Months

"And now, bless the God of all, who has done wonders on earth; Who fosters growth from the womb, fashioning it according to his will!"

-Sirach 50:22

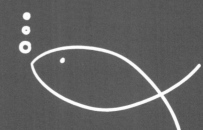

...& GREW!

7 Months

9 Months

8 Months

"Rather, living the truth in love, we should grow in every way into him who is the head, Christ."

-Ephesians 4:15

10 Months

11 Months

AND BEFORE WE KNEW IT, YOU WERE

1

Photo
3X5

1 Year Old!

CELEBRATING

2

2ⁿᵈ Birthday

3

3ʳᵈ Birthday

Photo
3X5

4ᵗʰ Birthday

5

Photo
3X5

5ᵗʰ Birthday

"For by me your days will be multiplied and the years of your life increased."

-Proverbs 9:11

FIRST DAY OF SCHOOL

"Listen to instruction and grow wise."

–Proverbs 8:33

GRADES K-2

Kindergarten   1ˢᵗ   2ⁿᵈ

YOU GREW IN YOUR FAITH

In kindergarten, you...   In first grade, you...   In second grade, you...

FIRST RECONCILIATION

"Have mercy on me, God, in accord with your merciful love; in your abundant compassion blot out my transgressions."

-Psalm 51:3

Photo 3X3

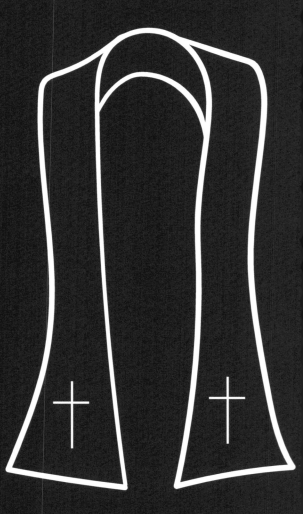

"Blessed is the one whose fault is removed, whose sin is forgiven."

—Psalm 32:1

First Holy Communion

"Whoever eats my flesh and drinks my blood has eternal life, and I will raise him on the last day. For my flesh is true food, and my blood is true drink."

-John 6:54-55

"Do this in memory of me."

-Luke 22:19

GRADES 3-5

3rd

4th

5th

YOU GREW IN YOUR FAITH

In third grade, you...

In fourth grade, you...

In fifth grade, you...

GRADES 6-8

6th   7th   8th

YOU GREW IN YOUR FAITH

In sixth grade, you...   In seventh grade, you...   In eighth grade, you...

CONFIRMATION

"But the one who gives us
security with you in Christ
and who anointed us is God;
he has also put his seal upon
us and given the Spirit in our
hearts as a first installment."

-2 Corinthians 1:21-22

CONFIRMED BY	DATE	CHURCH	SPONSOR

....

"Then they laid hands on them and they received the Holy Spirit."

–Acts 8:17

CONFIRMATION SAINT

_____

Pray for us!

GRADES 9-11

Photo
2.5X3.5

Photo
2.5X3.5

Photo
2.5X3.5

9th

10th

11th

YOU GREW IN YOUR FAITH

In ninth grade, you...

In tenth grade, you...

In eleventh grade, you...

SENIOR YEAR

"For I know well the plans I have in mind for you."

–Jeremiah 29:11

"Entrust your works to the LORD, and your plans will succeed."

–Proverbs 16:3

Photo 4X6

"We do not cease praying for you and asking that you may be filled with the knowledge of his will through all spiritual wisdom and understanding."

–Colossians 1:9

"And this is my prayer: that your love may increase ever more and more in knowledge and every kind of perception."

–Philippians 1:9

In twelfth grade, you...

ONWARD YOU GO

"Be strong and steadfast! Do not fear nor be dismayed, for the LORD, your God, is with you wherever you go."

—Joshua 1:9

A LETTER TO YOU

_____

_____

_____

_____

_____

_____

_____

_____

_____

_____

_____

_____

"We are inflamed, by Thy Gift we are kindled; and are carried upwards; we glow inwardly, and go forwards."

-Saint Augustine of Hippo

"Prayer is the door to those great graces which our Lord bestowed upon me."

-Saint Teresa of Ávila

"Oh, the great goodness and compassion of God! How He regards not the words, but the desire and the will with which they are spoken!"

-Saint Teresa of Ávila

"Honor, reverence, love, and respect in a special manner the sacred and glorious Virgin Mary, as she was the Mother of our sovereign Lord, so is she consequently our Mother."

–Saint Francis de Sales

"Make yourself familiar with the angels, and behold them frequently in spirit; for, without being seen, they are present with you."

-Saint Francis de Sales

"So we shall make our prayer continuous and faithful; because in the fire of His love we know that He is powerful to give us what we ask."

-Saint Catherine of Siena

"I want you to be now, kindled in the fire of divine charity, seeking always the honor of God and the salvation of souls."

-Saint Catherine of Siena

"So, each day I made a number of little sacrifices and acts of love, which were to be changed into so many flowers... all nature's blossoms were to form in me a cradle for the Holy Child."

-Saint Thérèse of Lisieux